The Rockwool Foundation Research Unit

A Panel Study of Immigrant Poverty Dynamics and Income Mobility – Denmark, 1984 – 2007

Peder J. Pedersen

University Press of Southern Denmark
Odense 2011

A Panel Study of Immigrant Poverty Dynamics
and Income Mobility – Denmark, 1984 – 2007

Study Paper No. 34

Published by:
© The Rockwool Foundation Research Unit and
University Press of Southern Denmark

Copying from this book is permitted only within
institutions that have agreements with CopyDan,
and only in accordance with the limitations laid
down in the agreement

Address:
The Rockwool Foundation Research Unit
Sølvgade 10
DK-1307 Copenhagen K

Telephone   +45 33 34 48 00

Fax   +45 33 34 48 99

E-mail   forskningsenheden@rff.dk

Home page   www.rff.dk

ISBN   978-87-90199-56-2
ISSN   0908-3979
May 2011
Print run: 300
Printed by   Specialtrykkeriet Viborg

Price: 60.00 DKK, including 25% VAT

Contents

Abstract 5
1. Introduction... 7
2. Earlier studies 8
3. Data, income concept and poverty line................... 9
   The data set 9
   The poverty line...................................... 9
4. Annual indicators of immigrant poverty, 1984 – 2007 9
5. Transitions between poverty and non-poverty, 1984 – 2007........ 18
6. Indicators of poverty persistence 24
7. Indicators of income mobility and inequality since 1984......... 28
8. Conclusions 34
Literature 36

A Panel Study of Immigrant Poverty Dynamics and Income Mobility – Denmark, 1984 – 2007[1]

Peder J. Pedersen
School of Economics and Management, Aarhus University

Abstract

In cross-country poverty studies Denmark, like the other Nordic countries, stands out with very low rates of poverty incidence and duration. The purpose in the present paper is to show that this is the net outcome of very different poverty profiles between natives and immigrants. We describe and analyse the annual incidence of poverty 1984 – 2007 separately for natives and for immigrants from Western and non-Western countries using panel data for the whole population. We further describe entry and exit rates relative to poverty and persistence of poverty for these three population groups. Finally, we calculate a set of indicators of income mobility and inequality for immigrant and native population groups.

JEL classifications: D31, F22, I32
Keywords: Poverty, Immigrants, Panel data

---

[1] The empirical part of this study is built on a micro panel data set made available by the Rockwool Foundation Research Unit. I am grateful for the opportunity to work with these data and grateful also for competent research assistance from Katrine Pedersen and Chalotte Bøgesvang. An earlier version of the paper was presented at the meeting in St. Gallen in 2010 in the International Association for Research in Income and Wealth. I am grateful for comments at the meeting and for constructive comments from a referee.

1. Introduction

In most cross-country studies, Denmark along with the other Nordic countries usually stand out with a very low level of poverty. This is the case in Fouarge and Layte (2005) working with data from the European Community Household Panel. They find not just a low level for the incidence of poverty in Denmark but find also that Denmark has the lowest level of persistent poverty, defined as at least 3 consecutive years in poverty. In Eurofound (2010) focus is on working poor in Europe and Denmark along with the Czech Republic is found to have the lowest level of working poor among the 27 member countries.

The purpose in the present study is to focus on the poverty situation in broad terms for immigrants in Denmark since 1984 based on individual panel data coming from administrative registers. The main finding is poverty indicators, especially for non-Western immigrants much higher than the record low level for the whole population. This is the case, both looking at single year poverty incidence and looking into indicators of poverty dynamics.

With a current population share for immigrants and descendants around 10 per cent, and 7 per cent looking only at immigrants and descendants coming from non-Western countries, this is a highly relevant issue in analyses and policy discussions of the Danish version of the Scandinavian/social democratic type of welfare state in the Esping-Andersen (1990) classification. In the following, Section 2 briefly presents a number of earlier – mainly Scandinavian – studies of immigrant poverty. Section 3 describes our data consisting of individual observations for the whole population, immigrants and natives, annually for the period 1984 – 2007. Section 3 also describes the income concept we are using as well as the choice of poverty or low income line. Focus in the remaining part of the paper is on a mainly descriptive analysis of several aspects of immigrant poverty benchmarked against natives. Focus in Section 4 is on the annual incidence of poverty. In Section 5 we look into transitions between states as poor and non-poor calculating entry rates to and exit rates from poverty. In Section 6 the issue is persistence of poverty, made operational by defining persistence as spending 3 consecutive years in poverty. Focus in Section 7 is on a set of indicators of upwards and downwards income mobility along with presentation of income inequality measures for a number of population groups. Finally, Section 8 concludes the paper.

2. Earlier studies

Fairly few more recent studies exist on the economic approach to poverty or low income in Denmark. The study by Pedersen and Smith (2000) focus on the low level of poverty in Denmark in a cross country context. The study contains a descriptive and analytical overview based on micro data covering the period 1980-1995. Separate information on immigrants status was however not available in this study. Economic Council (2006) contains a comprehensive empirical analysis of poverty including a brief section on immigrant poverty with emphasis on the fact that the situation for this group is quite different from the usual finding of low poverty incidence in Denmark in line with the findings in the present study.

Immigrant poverty – with focus on non-Western immigrants – is the topic in two comparative studies of Denmark and Sweden using comparable micro data sets, Blume et al. (2005), Blume et al. (2008). As the two countries to a great extent have the same labor market and welfare state characteristics, the focus in the two studies is on the differences in immigrants poverty that reflect big differences in arrival rates, years of residence, countries of origin and cyclical situation at time of arrival in the host country. Further studies of immigrant poverty in Sweden can be found in Ekberg (1994), Hammarstedt (2001) and Hammarstedt and Shukur (2007). In Galloway et al. (2009) the focus is on immigrant child poverty in a comparative study of Denmark, Norway and Sweden. Main findings are a much higher level of persistent poverty for children with a non-Western background than for native children. Further, the incidence of immigrant child poverty is higher in Denmark than in the two other countries. Finally, the high level of poverty incidence among immigrants in Denmark are emphasized in annual reports on poverty from the Business Council of the Labor Movement, most recently in a 2010 report on long-term poverty, cf Juul and Rosenlund (2010).

The main contribution in the present paper relative to earlier studies is the opportunity to base the analyses on a very long panel data set making it possible to gain new knowledge about the dynamics of poverty and about income distribution and mobility benchmarking immigrants against natives.

A well known factor of major importance regarding immigrants income is entry to the labor market in the host country. In Denmark, immigrant participation in the labor force has been increasing in the most recent years, but still to a level lower than for natives. Especially for female immigrants, participation rates are still much lower than for native women. The comprehensive income data used below are currently not updated beyond 2007. Available labor market evidence indicates that the crisis beginning in 2008 surprisingly has affected non-Western immigrants less than natives, cf. Pedersen (2011).

3. Data, income concept and poverty line

The data set

We are using a panel data set containing a multitude of demographic and economic variables for the whole population of Denmark. Data originate in administrative registers and the panel property is secured by use of a common personal identifier. The data in the present study covers the years 1984-2007. For immigrants the data set contains information on year of entry and country of origin and the same set of demographic and economic variables as for the rest of the population. The classification of persons into immigrants, descendants and natives follows the definitions applied by Statistics Denmark[2].

The poverty line

In order to construct our low-income line (or poverty line), in accordance with the recommendations in Atkinson et al. (2002), we use 60 per cent of the median in the distribution of equivalence adjusted disposable incomes as the cut off point. We use the OECD equivalence scale applied to disposable household incomes (including child support and subsidies to housing rents) to convert to individual incomes, i.e. the weight is 1.0 for first adult in household, 0.7 for other adult persons and 0.5 for every child. The equivalence scale adjusted household income is assigned to each member of the household and each household is assigned a weight equal to the number of members irrespective of age. As an example of this procedure, in a family consisting of two adults and two children, the household income is divided by 2,7 and the resulting amount is assigned to all 4 members in this household. In part of the analysis below we change the unit of analysis to a 3 year base defining poverty as being below 60 per cent of the median in the 3 years distribution of income.

4. Annual indicators of immigrant poverty, 1984 – 2007

The focus in this section is twofold. First, to describe the profile in the annual incidence of poverty or low income over nearly a quarter of a century with special emphasis on the situation for non-Western immigrants compared with Western immigrants and natives. Secondly, the section presents some initial analytical

---

2 The main division regarding countries of origin used by Statistics Denmark is between
  - Western countries consisting of the EU member states, Nordic countries outside the EU, Switzerland, Andorra, Liechtenstein, Monaco, San Marino, the Vatican State, Canada, USA, Australia and New Zealand
  - Non-Western countries: Rest of the World

results in the form of probit analyses of the risk of falling below the relative poverty line at four specific points in time over the period we cover, i.e. 1986, 1993, 2000 and 2007.

An aggregate picture of the incidence of annual poverty for the three population groups is shown in Figure 1. For native Danes we find a highly stable share around 12 per cent in the 25 – 59 years old group falling below 60 per cent of the median in the distribution of equivalence scale adjusted disposable incomes. This stability is surprising as the period under study contains very big cyclical movements, i.e. from 1986 to 1993 aggregate unemployment increases to an all times peak value while the years 1995 to 2007 show cyclical ups and downs to end with a near return to full employment by the end of the period. The surprising stability found for natives is the net outcome of a complex interaction between a decline in part-time participation among married women, an increase in female labor force participation in the first part of the period and the combined impact from taxes and public sector income supporting and replacing benefits.

On the contrary, stability is not what we see for the two groups of immigrants. For the broad group of immigrants from Western countries there is an increase from about 20 to about 30 per cent. The initial gap of about 8 percentage points relative to natives increases to nearly the double level around 16 percentage points. As Figure 1 covers individuals 25 – 59 years old the increasing gap is not related to for instance an increase in the number of students from other Western countries. We return to possible factors explaining the increasing gap below.

For immigrants (including refugees) from non-Western countries we find a completely different profile in the poverty share. From an initial level slightly below 30 per cent the share increases until the mid-1990s to a level close to 50 per cent of the group. During the last 10 years the level is stationary, moving between 45 and 50 per cent. This profile, and the widening gap relative to natives, is a reflection of the working of a multitude of factors. Changes occur in the composition of the group on countries of origin, waves of refugees arrive, the annual relative increase in the stock of immigrants is fast and as a consequence, the time of residence in Denmark is short for many in the group, and finally from the mid-1980s to the mid-1990s the inflow of immigrants and refugees was high at the same time as unemployment was high and increasing. The small decline from the peak in the poverty share in the mid-1990s until the turn of the century may reflect a cyclical upswing while the new increase in the poverty share may reflect policy changes enacted from 2000 which reduced cash benefits to some groups of new immigrants. We return to more detailed analyses and discussions below.

Figure 1. Annual incidence of low income. Share among immigrants from western and non-western countries, and natives with equivalence scale adjusted income under 60 per cent of the median income, 25 – 59 years old.

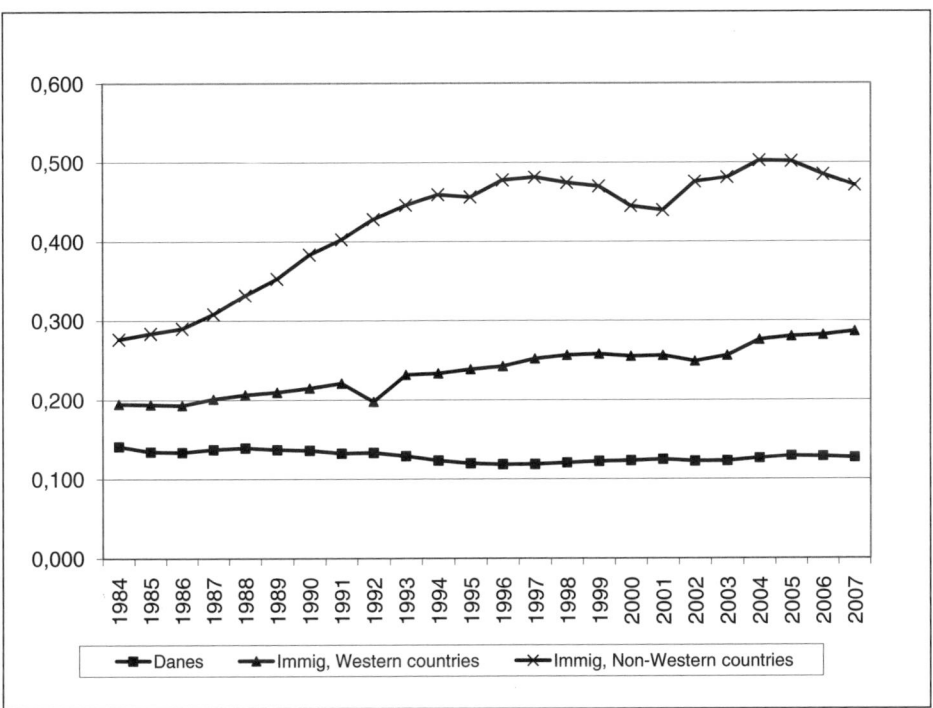

Figure 2 illustrates the variation between countries of origin showing poverty shares for individuals coming from two traditional guest worker nations, Turkey and Pakistan, along with people coming originally as refugees from Vietnam. While the gap narrows between people from Turkey and Pakistan, the level stabilizes between 50 and 60 per cent compared with respectively 30 and 40 per cent back in 1984. While the group from Vietnam follows the increasing trend in the poverty share during the deep recession from 1986 to 1993, an interesting break occurs in the years after 1993 where aggregate employment increases although with cyclical ups and downs.

Figure 2. Annual incidence of low income. Share among immigrants from three non-western countries with equivalence scale adjusted income under 60 per cent of the median income, 25 – 59 years old.

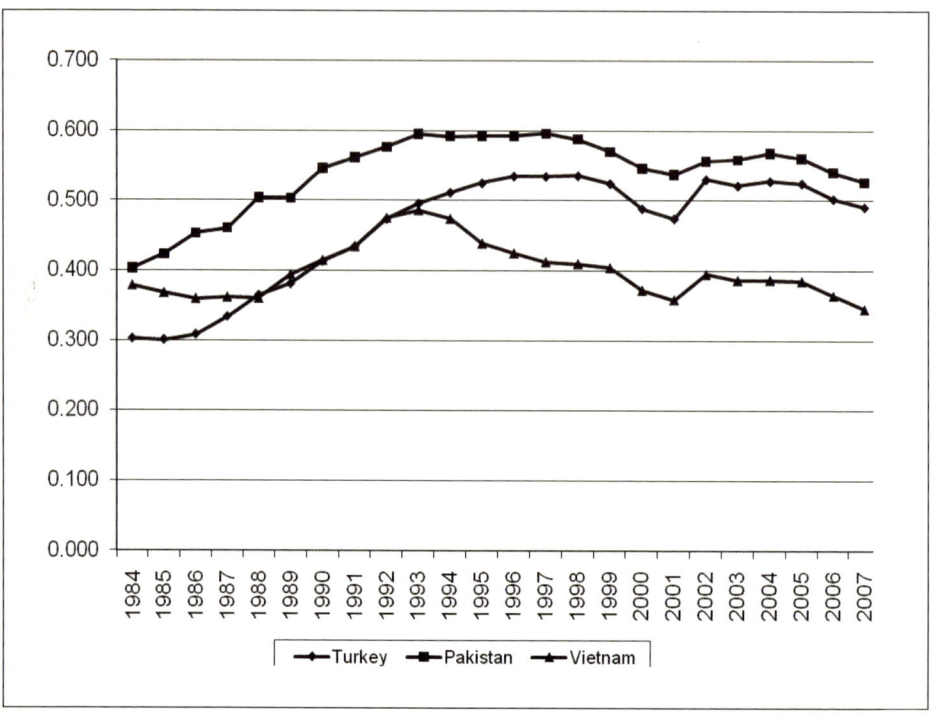

Tables 1 – 4 report the results from descriptive probit analyses of the risk of adjusted disposable income falling below 60 per cent of the median in 4 selected years 1986, 1993, 2000 and 2007 for all 25 – 59 years old in the 3 population groups. A long and deep recession began in 1986 with unemployment reaching a peak of 12 per cent in 1993. From 2003 unemployment goes down and employment goes up. The year 2000 marks a strong shift towards a much more restrictive policy regarding immigration from non-Western countries and regarding the Danish policy relative to receiving and granting asylum to refugees.

We include a battery of demographic variables along with an indicator for labor market attachment, a variable YSM measuring number of years since immigration and finally a number of specific countries of origin, for Western as well as non-Western immigrants.

Regarding the age profile in the poverty risk we find an interesting shift for non-Western immigrants from 1986 to the final year 2007. Initially, all age groups 30 and older have a higher poverty risk than the group younger than 30. This is in complete contrast to natives where the 25 – 29 years old consistently have a higher poverty risk than the older age groups. In 2007, the age profile for non-Western immigrants looks much more like the profile for natives for those in the core age groups 30 – 49.

For gender we find no strong or consistent pattern relative to the poverty risk. In the second half of the period, women tend to have a higher poverty risk in both the non-Western and the native groups. Civil status is measured using 3 different dummy variables. For non-Western immigrants Married_1 is set at 1 if the individual is married (or cohabiting), Married_2 is set at 1 if the individual is married to a native and Married_3 is set at 1 for an individual married to a Western immigrant. For Western immigrants the dummy variables are defined in a parallel way. Finally, for natives, Married_2 is set at 1 for an individual married to a Western immigrant while Married_3 is set at 1 if the individual is married to a non-Western immigrant. Overall, being married or cohabiting as expected reduces the poverty risk. For both non-Western and Western immigrants this is reinforced if the marriage is to a native.

For all 3 groups, having children, younger as well as older, increases the poverty risk. Education and labor force attachment both have the expected significantly negative impact on the probability of poverty with labor force attachment consistently having a much higher coefficient. In all 4 years, the number of years since immigration has a significant negative impact on the poverty risk, i.e. immigrants integrate out of poverty. This, however, as indicated in Figures 1 and 2 does not imply a low *level* of the poverty share.

Tables 1-4 report also the coefficients to a number of specific countries of origin for Western as well as for non-Western immigrants. The composition of immigrants on countries of origin shifts quite much, especially for the non-Western group, implying that the same countries only in a small number of cases are included in all 4 years. Taking 2007 as an example, for non-Western immigrants the excluded country is Iran.[3] So, the results show significantly higher poverty risk compared with immigrants from Iran for people coming from Turkey, Pakistan, Iraq, Lebanon and Somalia while immigrants from Bosnia have a significantly lower risk compared with people from Iran. For Western immigrants we also find big cross-country differences. For the – fairly few – countries included in all 4 estimations we find a trend from lower to higher poverty risk compared with the excluded country in this group.

---

3 For 1986 the excluded countries are India and France. For 1993 it is Sri Lanka and the Netherlands, for 2000 it is Somalia and Finland and finally for 2007 it is, cf. above Iran and Finland.

Table 1. Probit analyses of the incidence of poverty, Non-Western and Western immigrants and natives, 25 – 59 years old, 1986.

Variables	Non-Western		Western		Natives	
	Coefficient	Z value	Coefficient	Z value	Coefficient	Z value
Constant	0.1521	2.19	0.8880	13.16	-0.4562	-6.31
Gender	0.0248	1.11	0.0179	0.91	-0.0195	-7.64
Age 30-39	0.0114	4.66	-0.1487	-6.22	-0.1634	-41.06
Age 40-49	0.2997	9.12	-0.2207	-7.31	-0.1014	-23.78
Age 50-59	0.5063	11.33	-0.4653	-11.05	-0.0209	-4.64
Married_1	-0.8076	-27.93	-0.7445	-18.20	-0.6493	-109.66
Married_2	-0.1510	-4.32	-0.3747	-8.89	-0.2074	-35.11
Married_3	0.1152	1.34	0.0759	1.72	-0.0747	-6.06
Child 0_6	0.3967	29.23	0.3353	21.28	0.3927	164.88
Child 7_17	0.3446	30.35	0.2955	19.99	0.4056	243,67
Education	-0.0287	-15.17	-0.0429	-26.87	-0.0480	-114.04
Labor force	-0.6437	-28.70	-0.6431	-29.33	-0.6021	-174.55
YSM	-0.0238	-7.98	-0.0487	-18.25	-	-
Turkey	-0.5058	-8.16	-	-	-	-
Pakistan	0.0658	1.04	-	-	-	-
Vietnam	0.6785	2.50	-	-	-	-
Morocco	-0.1143	-1.42	-	-	-	-
Soviet Union	0.3348	3.32	-	-	-	-
Other non-W	-0.1917	-3.26	-	-	-	-
Germany			-0.0859	-1.44	-	-
Sweden			-0.1305	-2.13	-	-
Norway			-0.0057	-0.09	-	-
UK			-0.2108	-3.44	-	-
USA			0.1870	2.83	-	-
Finland			-0.1477	-2.01	-	-
Iceland			0.0458	0.08	-	-
Other W			-0.0273	-0.48	-	-
No. of obs.	22054		25465		2239418	
Pseudo R^2	0.1746		0.2005		0.1242	

Table 2. Probit analyses of the incidence of poverty, Non-Western and Western immigrants and natives, 25 – 59 years old, 1993.

Variables	Non-Western		Western		Natives	
	Coefficient	Z value	Coefficient	Z value	Coefficient	Z value
Constant	0.6807	25.15	1.2114	22.80	-0.0048	-0.70
Gender	-0.8887	-6.78	0.0067	0.42	0.0042	1.66
Age 30-39	-0.0216	-1.45	-0.1761	-8.20	-0.2316	-62.44
Age 40-49	0.1145	5.67	-0.1894	-7.60	-0.2409	-61.47
Age 50-59	0.3071	11.04	-0.2515	-7.99	-0.2177	-51.10
Married_1	-0.9461	-55.28	-0.7486	-22.11	-0.7179	-115.18
Married_2	-0.3909	-18.01	-0.4641	-13.51	-0.2455	-38.89
Married_3	0.0655	1.19	0.0709	1.94	0.0403	3.37
Child 0_6	0.5278	62.64	0.3114	24.62	0-3933	180.67
Child 7_17	0.5058	70.98	0.3528	30.28	0.4135	233.62
Education	-0.0249	-21.77	-0.3963	-29.76	-0.0388	-94.38
Labor force	-0.7905	-59,22	-0.7202	-40.17	-0.5950	-178.44
YSM	-0.0431	-32.49	-0.0448	-28.72	-	-
Turkey	0.0080	0.39	-	-	-	-
Pakistan	0.4388	16.87	-	-	-	-
Marocco	-0.0372	-1.03	-	-	-	-
Soviet Union	0.1425	2.34	-	-	-	-
Other non-W	0.1572	9.92	-	-	-	-
Germany	-	-	-0.1528	-3.32	-	-
Sweden	-	-	-0.2568	-5.31	-	-
Norway	-	-	-0.1785	-3.73	-	-
UK	-	-	-0.2107	-4.49	-	-
USA	-	-	0.0273	0.52	-	-
Finland	-	-	-0.2314	-3.84	-	-
Iceland	-	-	0.1298	0.31	-	-
Other W	-	-	-0.0492	-1.14	-	-
No. of obs.	56732		37954		2381718	
Pseudo R^2	0.2509		0.2349		0.1475	

Table 3. Probit analyses of the incidence of poverty, Non-Western and Western immigrants and natives, 25 – 59 years old, 2000.

Variables	Non-Western		Western		Natives	
	Coefficient	Z value	Coefficient	Z value	Coefficient	Z value
Constant	0.6755	23.71	0.9533	19.12	-0.0881	-12.96
Gender	-0.0047	-0.50	0.0144	1.10	0.0401	16.14
Age 30-39	-0.1079	-8.78	-0.2790	-14.92	-0.3425	-90.36
Age 40-49	0.0268	1.81	-0.3276	-15.42	-0.4295	-104.76
Age 50-59	0.2135	10.94	-0.2339	-9.66	-0.3411	-81.27
Married_1	-1.0468	-82.24	-0.5830	-20.68	-0.5875	-96.64
Married_2	-0.3997	-24.51	-0.6064	-21.08	-0.4025	-65.27
Married_3	0.1774	4.08	0.0396	1.31	-0.0281	-2.48
Child 0_6	0.7971	115.90	0.4239	39.50	0.5603	270.83
Child 7_17	0.7491	124.00	0.4568	48.83	0.5729	333,55
Education	-0.0229	-24.66	-0.0271	-21.56	-0.0369	-91.52
Labor force	-0.7691	-76.04	-0.8155	-54.03	-0.6059	-182.97
YSM	-0.0319	-40.14	-0.0323	-31.60		
Turkey	0.0016	0.06				
Pakistan	0.2095	7.13				
Bosnia	-0.4917	-18.33				
Lebanon	0.1513	5.07				
Yugoslavia	-0.0627	-0.62				
Iran	0.0103	0.37				
Other non-W	-0.0870	-3.82				
Germany			-0.0059	-0.14		
Sweden			-0.0332	-0.74		
Norway			0.0640	1.43		
UK			0.0483	1.09		
USA			0.2680	5.54		
Iceland			-0.5711	-0.77		
Netherlands			0.3140	6.34		
Other W			0.1369	3.30		
No. of obs.	110740		55292		2463923	
Pseudo R^2	0.3214		0.2238		0.1868	

Table 4. Probit analyses of the incidence of poverty, Non-Western and Western immigrants and natives, 25 – 59 years old, 2007.

Variables	Non-Western		Western		Natives	
	Coefficient	Z value	Coefficient	Z value	Coefficient	Z value
Constant	0.7377	31.17	1.0505	19.84	0.4039	59.17
Gender	0.0562	7.30	-0.0022	-0.17	0.0687	26.40
Age 30-39	-0.1583	-14.09	-0.3477	-18.71	-0.5071	-128.92
Age 40-49	-0.0998	-8.01	-0.4822	-23.30	-0.7485	-177.78
Age 50-59	0.0181	1.20	-0.5290	-22.42	-0.9042	-196.13
Married_1	-0.6733	-67.40	-0.5600	-20.80	-0.6267	-100.35
Married_2	-0.7758	-54.43	-0.6842	-24.45	-0.5787	-89.53
Married_3	-0.2202	-5.66	-0.0985	-3.34	-0.1845	-15.24
Child 0_6	0.6976	113.12	0.4352	40.20	0.5606	255.95
Child 7_17	0.6432	132.29	0.4271	47.40	0.5789	328.18
Education	-0.0224	-29.32	-0.0266	-22.90	-0.0388	-103.47
Labor force	-0.9319	-104.49	-1.2001	-82.58	-0.7781	-218.62
YSM	-0.0232	-4114	-0.0157	-16.68		
Turkey	0.1312	7.01				
Pakistan	0.1004	4.40				
Iraq	0.3115	14.69				
Lebanon	0.3366	14.18				
Bosnia	-0.4681	-21.80				
Somalia	0.2248	8.42				
Ex-Yugosl.	-0.0710	-1.38				
Other non-W	-0.0292	-1.74				
Germany			0.1206	2.52		
Sweden			0.0669	1.34		
Norway			0.0712	1.44		
UK			0.1491	3.02		
USA			0.3206	6.04		
Netherlands			0.1735	3.26		
Other W			0.2272	4.93		
No. of obs.	152582		64502		2335640	
Pseudo R^2	0.2974		0.2965		0.2346	

5. Transitions between poverty and non-poverty, 1984 – 2007

The welfare consequences of poverty depends on a multitude of factors, i.e. the severity of the situation measured by the distance from a given level of income to the poverty line, the duration of poverty spells and the eventual recurrence of poverty. It is obvious that a brief spell of poverty experienced once in a life time is completely different from a situation characterized by long spells of poverty experienced many times during a persons life.

In this section we look into one aspect of the dynamics of poverty, i.e. the entry rates to, respectively the exit rates from poverty over the long period 1984-2007. In Figure 3 we show the average annual entry rates to a state with adjusted income below 60 per cent of the median. We calculate the entry rate as the number of transitions from t to t+1 from having an adjusted income above 60 per cent of the median to having an income below the poverty line in t+1 relative to the number of people having an income above the poverty line in period t.

Figure 3. Annual entry rates to low income, 1984 – 2007. Western and Non-Western immigrants and natives.

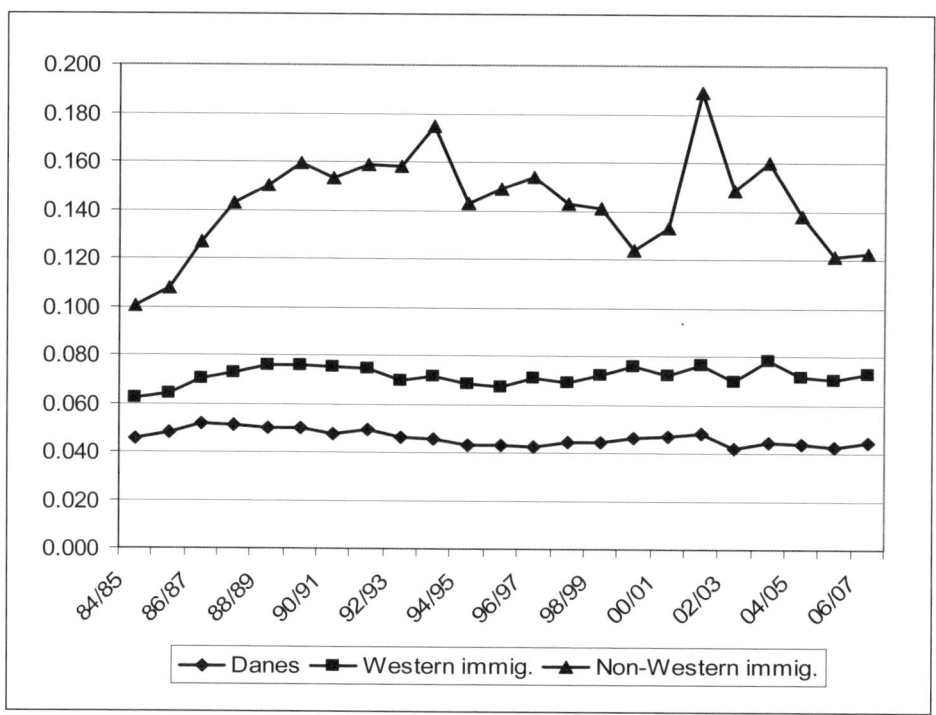

For natives and for Western immigrants the annual entry rates are stationary over the period. For natives, 25 – 59 years old, the entry rate is between 4 and 5 per cent, and for Western immigrants the entry rate is between 7 and 8 per cent. For non-Western immigrants the story is completely different as shown in Figure 3. The initial level is 10 per cent, only slightly higher than the two other groups, but this is followed by a steep increase to a peak of 18 per cent in 1994. This period of strong increase is, as mentioned above, years of increasing unemployment up to a peak in 1993 and at the same time a period with a big inflow of refugees and tied movers. The immigration profile is assumed to be important as natives have entry rates that seem to be unaffected by the long and deep recession. From 1994 unemployment goes down from 12 per cent to 5 per cent in 2002. During these years the entry rate follows unemployment down, nearly returning to the initial level in 1984 in spite of the fact that big flows of refugees arrive from Bosnia in the mid-1990s[4]. Next, the sharp increase in the entry rate from 1999 to 2002 seems to be a reflection of a number of policy changes with cut backs in social assistance, having their main impact on immigrants from non-Western countries, see Pedersen (2010). Finally, from 2004 unemployment once again goes down to a level below 3 per cent in 2007 and the entry rate to poverty for non-Western immigrants returns to a level only slightly above the initial level in 1984.

The exit rates are shown in Figure 4. They are calculated as the number of transitions from t to t+1 from having an adjusted income below 60 per cent of the median to having an income above this level, relative to the number of individuals with incomes below the poverty line in period t. We find the reverse ranking between the groups relative to the ranking of entry rates. Natives have the highest exit rates at a stable level between 30 and 35 per cent that seems to be completely independent of cyclical movements in the economy. For Western immigrants we find a somewhat surprising profile as the exit rate *declines* from the mid-1990s, i.e. in the period where unemployment goes down steeply. The increasing poverty share for Western immigrants shown in Figure 1 is a reflection of the stable entry rate in Figure 3 and the decline to a lower level for the exit rate found in Figure 4. More detailed analyses are necessary to determine how the decline in the exit rate relates to changes in the flows and stock of Western immigrants by country of origin, age, education and propensity to return migrate.

For the group of non-Western immigrants a "stylized" picture of the observations in Figure 4 is a decline in steps for the exit rate. The first stage is the 1980s with exit rates slightly above 20 per cent. Then a decline occurs to a new level of 15-16 per cent in the second half of the 1990s. Finally, a still lower level is seen for the years after the turn of the century.

---

[4] Newly arrived immigrants are included in the calculations from the first full calendar year of residence in Denmark.

Figure 4. Annual exit rates from low income, 1984 – 2007. Western and Non-Western immigrants and natives.

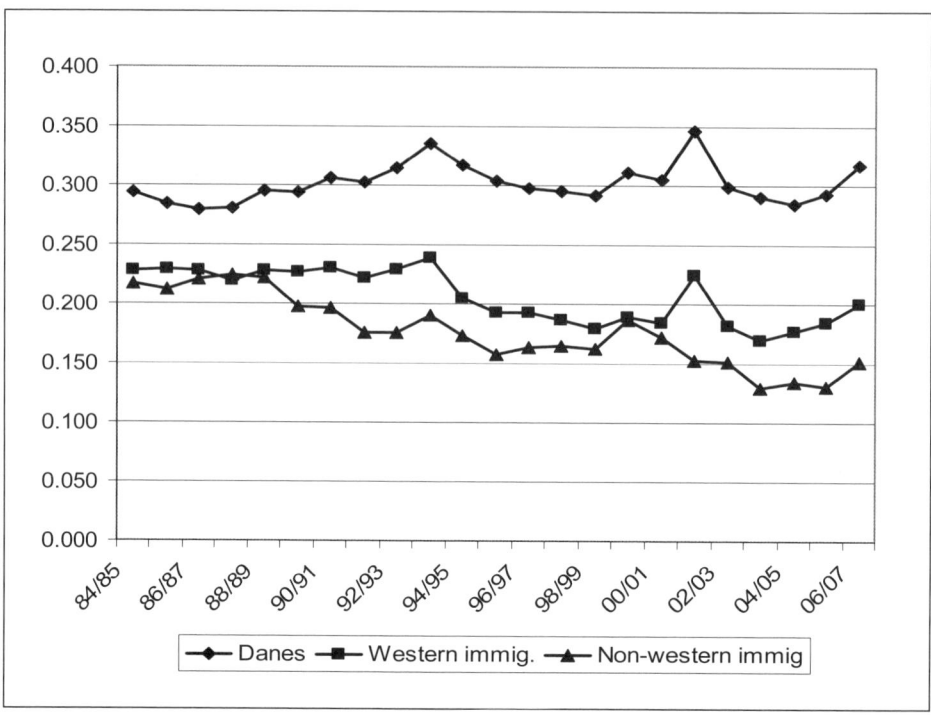

For immigrants from the 3 countries Turkey, Pakistan and Vietnam for whom poverty shares were shown in Figure 2, we show annual entry and exit rates in Figures 5 and 6. For Turkey and Pakistan entry rates are increasing until the mid-1990s while exit rates are stable from the early 1990s, both in accordance with poverty shares increasing to a stable high level in Figure 2. For Vietnam, the falling poverty share from the early 1990s is the net outcome of a steep decline in the entry rate and a stable exit rate.

Figure 5. Annual entry rates to low income, 1984 – 2007. Immigrants from Turkey, Pakistan and Vietnam.

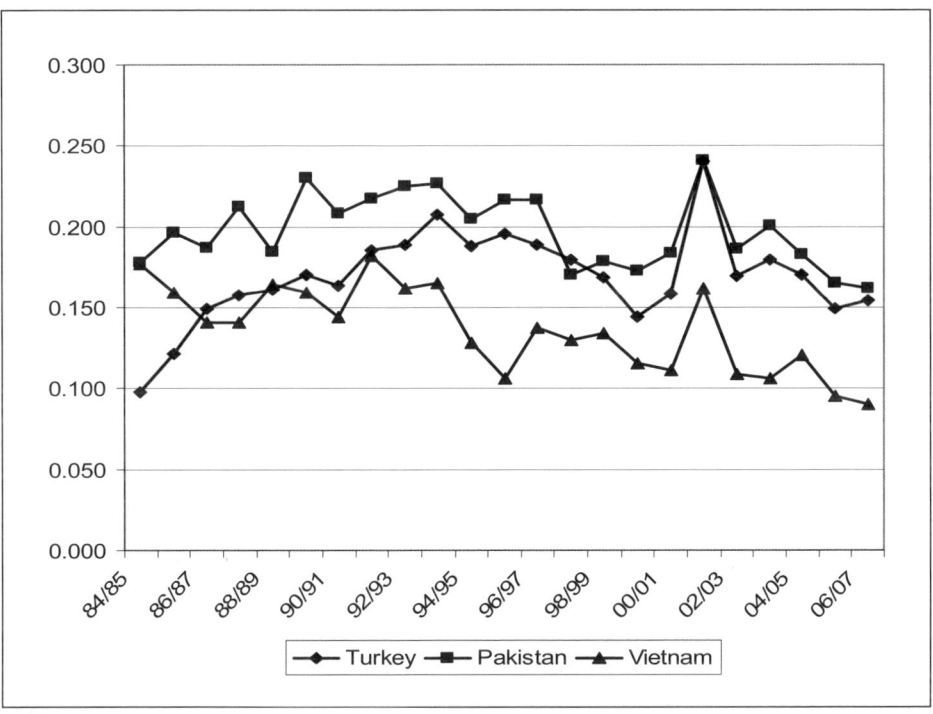

Figure 6. Annual exit rates from low income, 1984 – 2007. Immigrants from Turkey, Pakistan and Vietnam.

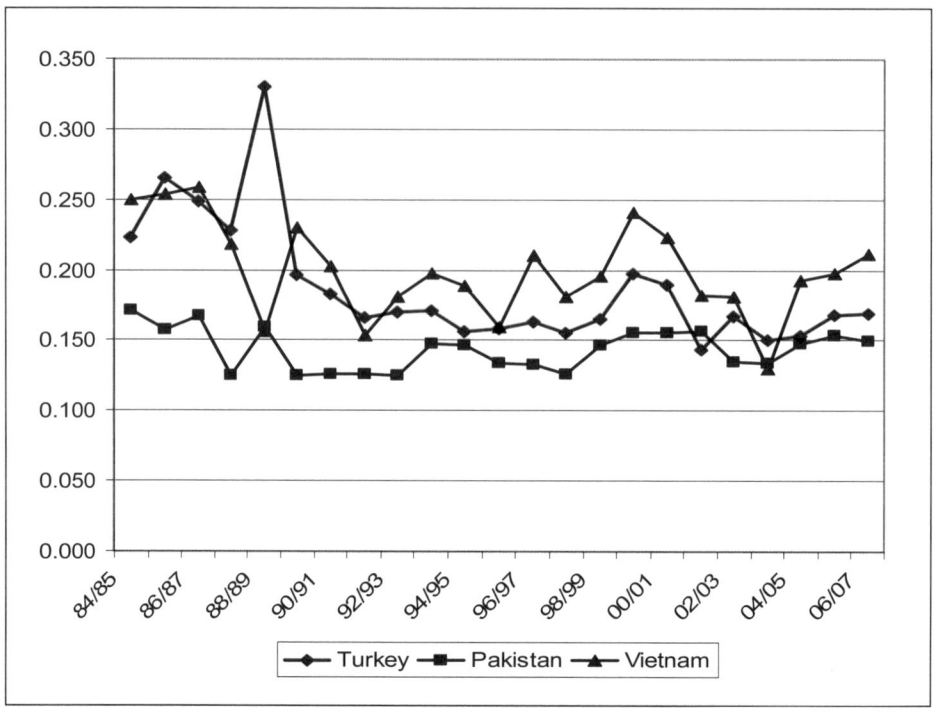

While Figures 4 and 6 illustrate the exit rate from poverty, Figure 7 shows a special aspect of the persistence of poverty. For each of 3 years in the period we study, 1986, 1993 and 2002, we construct Kaplan Meier graphs showing the share of people initially in poverty in the sected years who are also poor in subsequent years. For 1986 we select all 25-49 years old non-Western immigrants with YSM=2 in 1986, and who stays in the country in each of the next 10 years until 1996, conditional on being below the poverty line in 1986. In each of the subsequent 10 years we find the number of people in this initial population who are below the poverty line and and calculate the ratio relative to the initial population[5].

---

5 This is an approximative survival curve as some individuals in the population may be out of poverty in some of the years and then return to a position below the line.

The same exercise is made for 1993 and for 2002 where only observations for 6 years are available. While 80 per cent of the initially poor in 1986, who arrived in 1984, are out of poverty 5 years later, the situation has deteriorated significantly for the 1993 cohort, arriving in 1991. For this cohort, only 60 per cent have left poverty after 5 years and after 11 years 20 per cent are still in poverty in contrast to the 1986 cohort where nearly all initially poor have left poverty. Finally, the 2002 cohort, arriving in 2000, has a profile very close to the 1993 cohort as far as the observations go.

Summing up, identifying the more specific factors behind the Kaplan-Meier curves, it would be necessary to go into more details regarding arrival patterns between 1984 and 1991 regarding numbers, countries of origin and whether arrival was as tied movers or as refugees. When comparing 1993 and 2002, it is interesting to notice that the big inflow of refugees from Bosnia and other countries in the mid-1990s, the cuts in benefit programs with special impact on immigrants and the more restrictive immigration policy does not result in a new move outwards of the Kaplan-Meier curve.

Figure 7. Kaplan-Meier graphs for non-western immigrants surviving in a state of low income. Initial years 1986, 1993 and 2002.

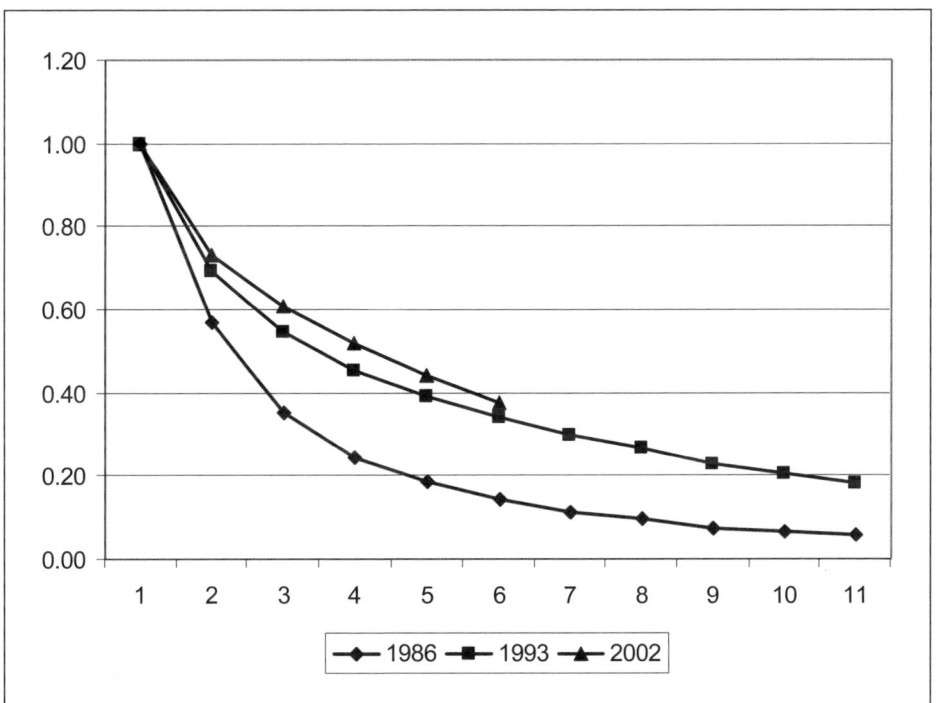

6. Indicators of poverty persistence

The purpose in this Section is to present some preliminary indicators of poverty persistence for non-Western immigrants benchmarked against natives. First, we present distributions of the number of years spent in poverty going from 0 to 12 in each of two sub-periods, 1984 – 1995 and 1996 – 2007. Next, we "define" persistence of poverty as being poor for 3 consecutive years. We use the same sub-periods 1984 – 1995 and 1996 – 2007. In each of these periods individuals could experience from 0 to 4 spells of persistent poverty, each of 3 years duration where each of the 3 years is spent in poverty.

The sample used in this context is

- All non-Western immigrants who are between 18 and 48 years old in 1984, respectively in 1996

- And who are residents in the country in each of the years from 1984 to 1995, respectively in each of the years from 1996 to 2007.

The same selection rule applies to natives. For both groups we calculate equivalence scale adjusted incomes as the sum of incomes over the 3 years. The poverty line is 60 per cent of the median in the distribution of the 3 years incomes for all in each 3 year period.

First, we present in Figure 8 the distribution of number of years spent in poverty for non-Western immigrants, respectively for natives for the most recent sub-period 1996 – 2007[6].

---

6 The corresponding graph is available for the period 1984 – 1995.

Figure 8. Distribution of number of years spent in poverty, 1996-2007, for non-Western immigrants and natives.

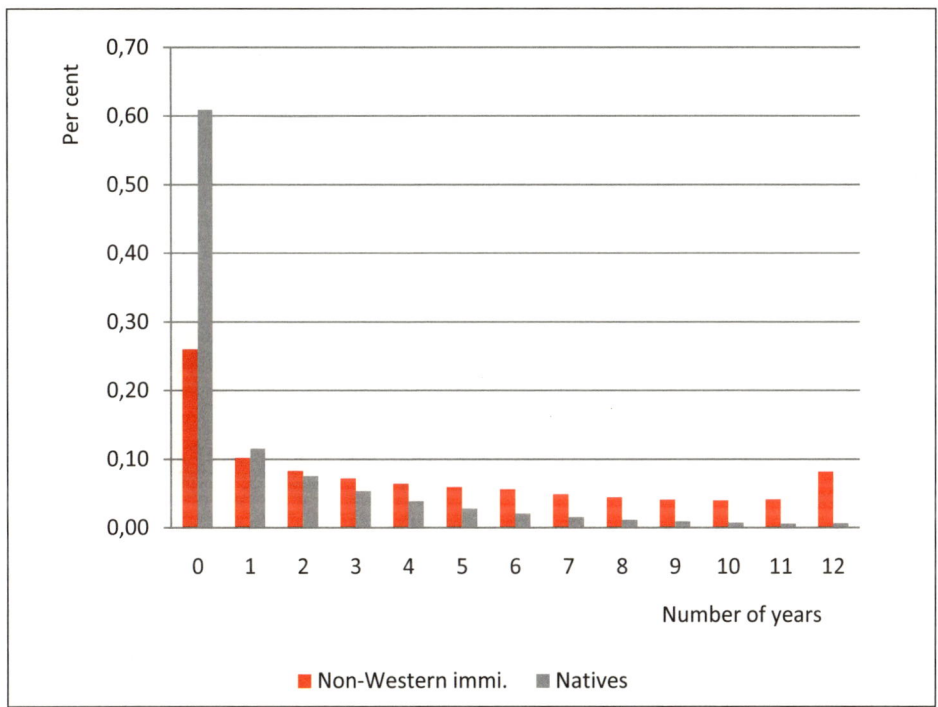

While 60 per cent of the natives do not experience a year with poverty, this is so for only about 25 per cent of the non-Western immigrants. In the opposite end of the distribution about 20 per cent of the immigrants spend 9 or more years in poverty against 3 per cent in the native group.

Figure 9. Distribution of number of years spent in poverty for non-Western immigrants in 1984-1995 and 1996-2007.

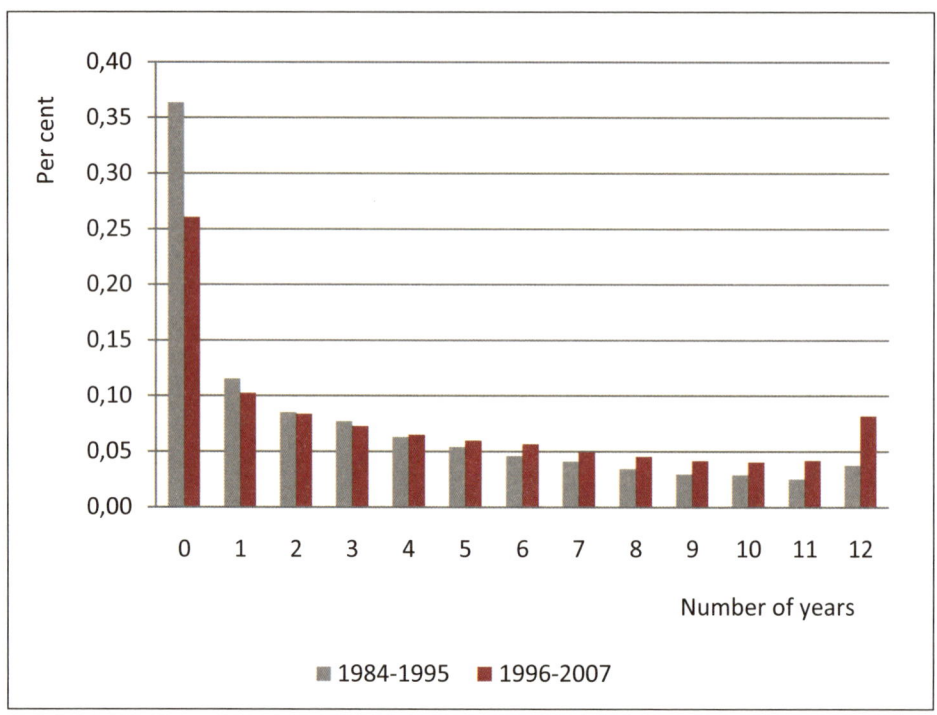

Another dimension is shown in Figure 9 comparing the distribution of number of years in poverty for non-Western immigrants across the two time periods. The profile found here confirms finding from earlier sections in the paper, i.e. the poverty situation has become worse for immigrants over the last quarter of a century.

A more explicit approach to persistence is, as mentioned, to change focus to use 3 consecutive years as the unit of measurement. The outcome in each of the two sub-periods is then from 0 to being persistently poor in each of the four 3-year periods. In Figure 10 we benchmark the distribution for non-Western immigrants against natives for the most recent sub-period[7].

---

7 The corresponding graph is available for the period 1984 – 1995.

Figure 10. Distribution on number of spells with 3 consecutive years in poverty, 1996-2007, for non-Western immigrants and natives.

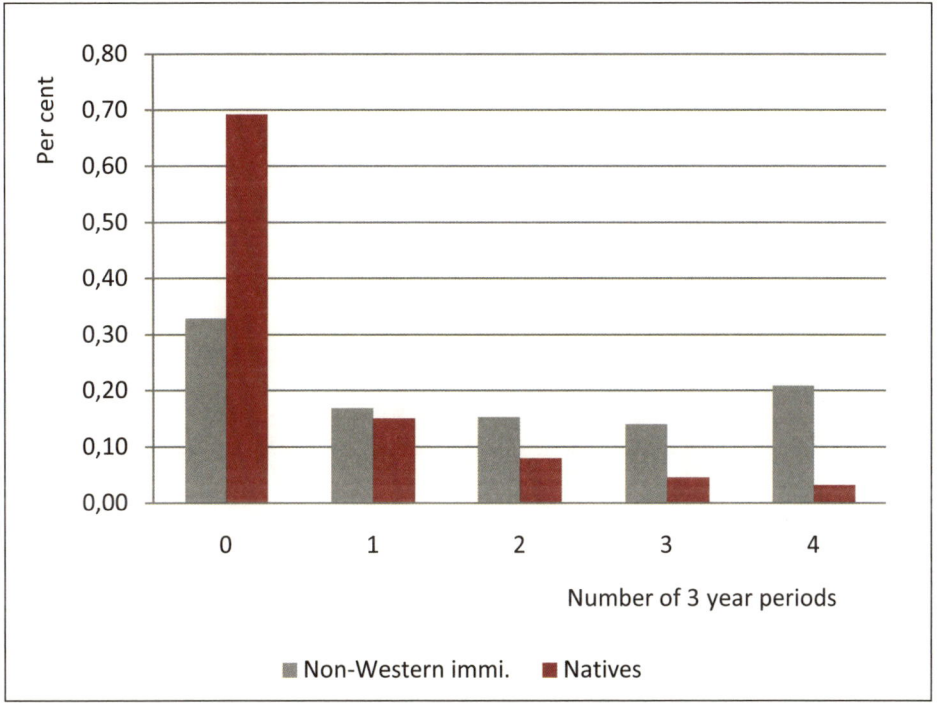

Again, we find an impressive difference between the two groups, i.e. while 70 per cent in the group of natives do not have any spell of persistent poverty, this is only so for just over 30 per cent of the immigrants group. At the other end, one third of the immigrants have 3 or more spells of persistent poverty and 20 per cent are living in persistent poverty in all of the 3 year periods. Finally, Figure 11 compares the distributions for non-Western immigrants across the two sub-periods. We find a dramatic decline in the share having no spell of persistent poverty and a corresponding dramatic doubling from 10 to 20 per cent having 4 spells of persistent poverty.

6. Indicators of poverty persistence

Figure 11. Distribution on number of poverty spells with 3 consecutive years in poverty for non-Western immigrants, 1984-1995 and 1996-2007.

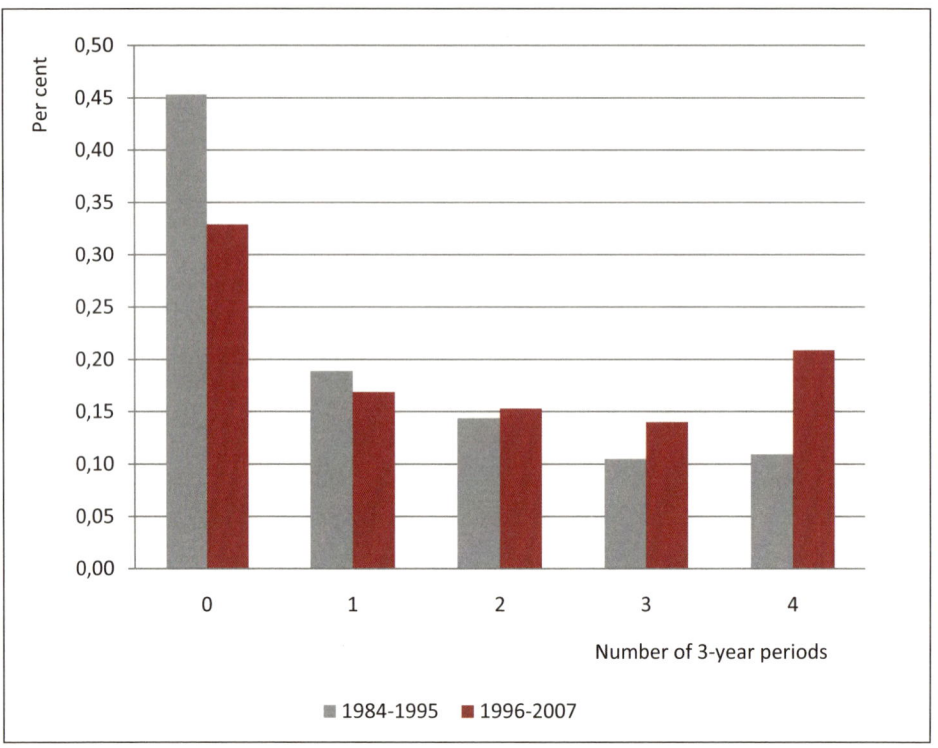

7. Indicators of income mobility and inequality since 1984

In this section we will illustrate income mobility in the 3 population groups in different ways. We focus first on a mobility indicator over the long span from 1984 to 2006. Next, we focus on current income mobility for immigrants from a number of important non-Western countries. Another dimension is an illustration of the dependence of income mobility on the number of years since immigration. Finally, we look into inequality aspects in the distribution of current income for the 3 population groups by calculating Gini coefficients. The focus is throughout on equivalence scale adjusted disposable incomes for people 25 – 59 years old to exclude as much as possible the importance of students and of early retirement.

First, Figure 12 shows an indicator for upwards income mobility for the 3 population groups annually from 1984 to 2006. We measure upwards mobility by the share of people in the 2. quintile in year t who in year t+1 has moved to the 4. or the 5. quintile, i.e. those who have moved up at least 2 quintiles.

Figure 12. Indicator of annual upwards mobility of adjusted disposable income, 25 – 59 years old, Western and non-Western immigrants and natives.

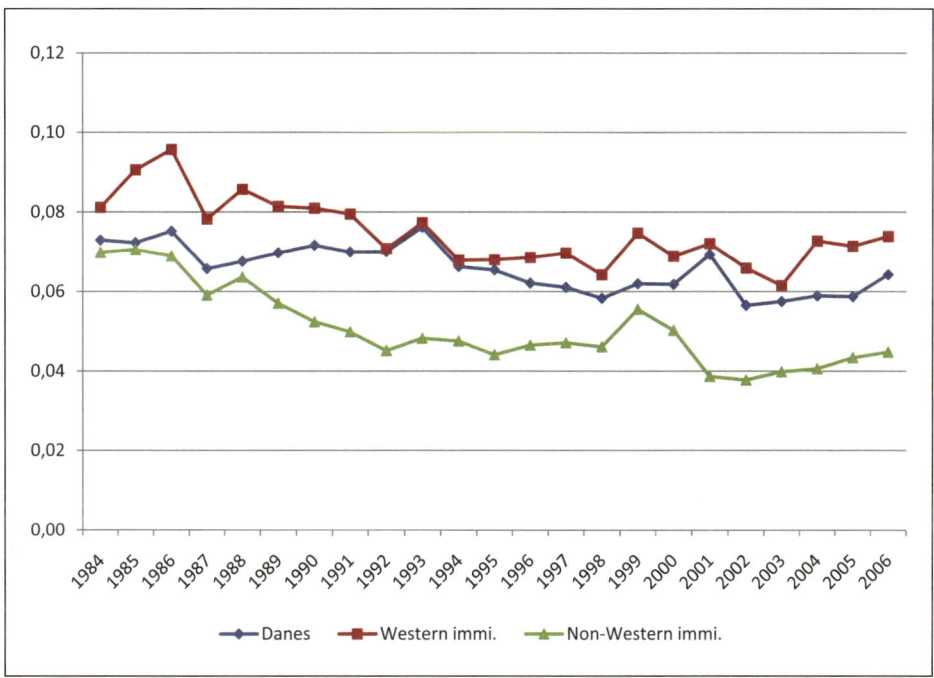

For the two groups of immigrants, this measure of mobility is trending down throughout the deep recession until 1993. The mobility indicator becomes stationary in the recovery years towards the turn of the century and increases during the strong cyclical improvement after 2000. For non-Western immigrants the increase is very moderate. For natives, there is little variation around a decline in the level of upwards mobility from 7 to 6 per cent. Looking at the situation for non-Western immigrants relative to natives, we find a clear deterioration from close to parity in the beginning of the period to a situation where immigrant mobility is down to about 70 per cent of the level for natives.

Income mobility downwards is measured in a parallel way as the relative share of people in the 4. quintile in year t who in year t+1 are in the 1. or the 2. quintile, i.e. have moved down at least 2 quintiles. The results for the 3 groups are shown in Figure 13. The levels are stationary for natives at around 7 per cent and for Western immigrants around 10 per cent. For non-Western immigrants, the indicator shows increasing downwards mobility until the cyclical bottom in 1993 followed by a fall to about half the peak level in 2006. Notice a jump up in the indicator around the turn of the century coincident with cutbacks in benefit programs of special importance for immigrants.

Figure 13. Indicator of annual downwards mobility of adjusted disposable income, 25 – 59 years old, Western and non-Western immigrants and natives.

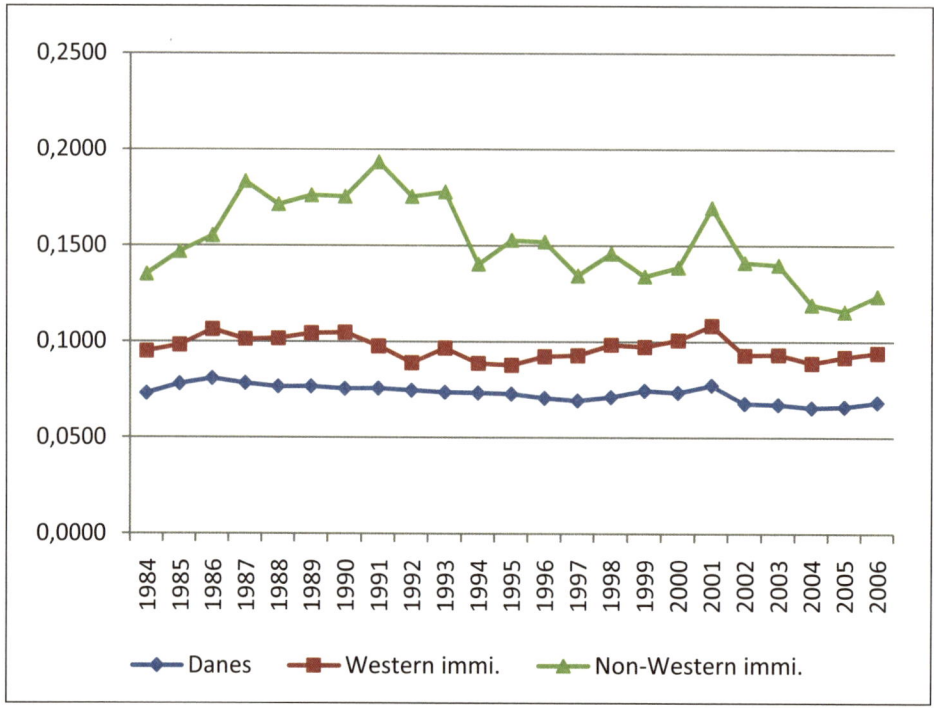

Using the most recent data Figure 14 shows the same indicators for upwards and downwards mobility from 2006 to 2007 for immigrants from 6 non-Western countries. There is fairly little variation in the rate of upwards mobility. Downwards mobility, on the other hand, is characterized by big variation between a low of 6 per cent for people from Bosnia and a peak of about 28 per cent for people coming from Somalia.

Figure 14. Mobility indicators for immigrants from 6 non-western countries from 2006 to 2007. Upwards mobility measured as relative share of individuals in 2. quintile in 2006 who moves to 4. or 5. quintile in 2007. Downwards mobility measured as relative share of individuals in 4. quintile in 2006 who moves to 1. or 2. quintile in 2007.

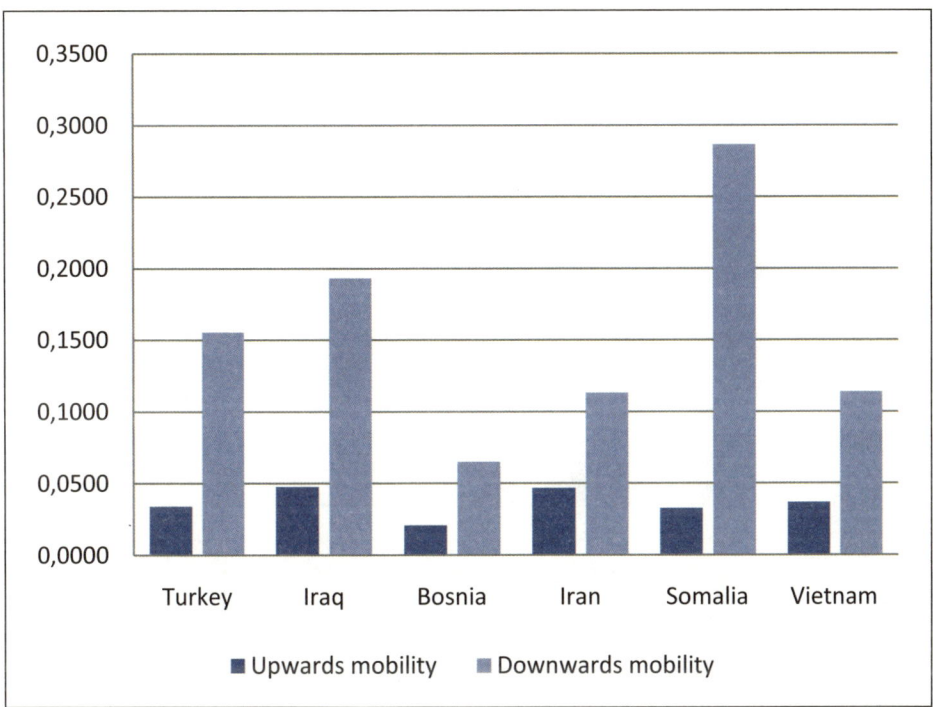

Next, Figure 15 shows the two mobility indicators 2006-2007 for immigrants from non-Western countries by the number of years since immigration going from newly arrived to people with 21 and more years of residence since arrival. Upwards mobility is decreasing over the first 10 years of residence followed by a stable level. The downwards mobility indicator declines with YSM, but not very much, and remains significantly higher than the level for natives also for immigrants with more than 20 years of residence, cf. Figure 15.

Figure 15. Mobility indicators for immigrants from Non-Western countries from 2006 to 2007 by number of years since immigration. Upwards mobility measured as relative share of individuals in 2. quintile in 2006 who moves to 4. or 5. quintile in 2007. Downwards mobility measured as relative share of individuals in 4. quintile in 2006 who moves to 1. or 2. quintile in 2007.

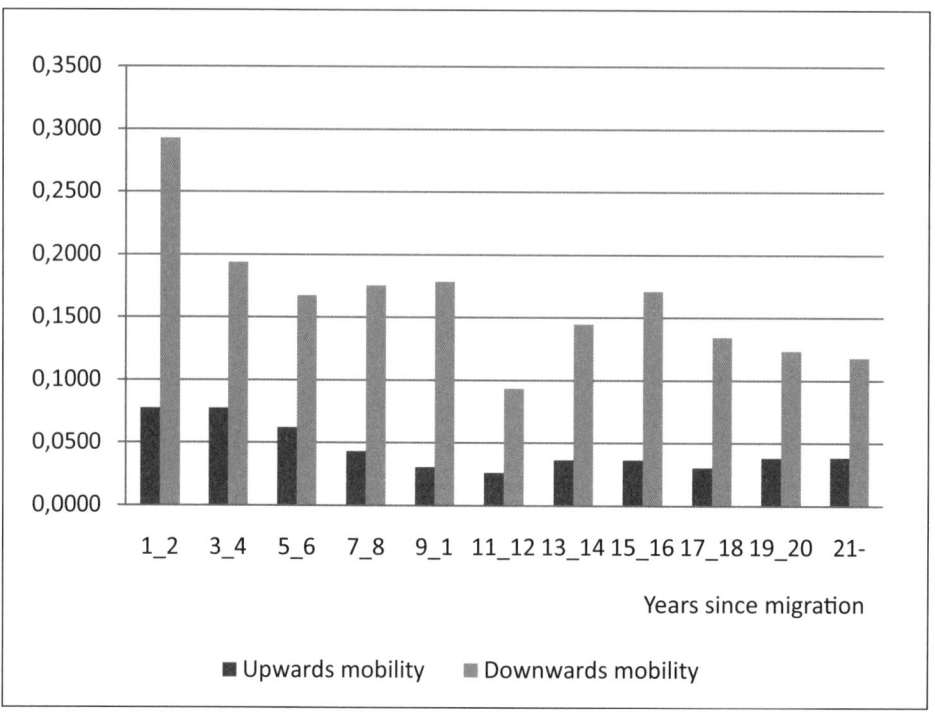

Next, we illustrate inequality in the income distribution for the 3 population groups. In Figure 16 we show Gini coefficients for each year 1984 to 2007 for the 18 – 66 years old. For natives, inequality is increasing beginning around the cyclical turning point in 1993. Inequality is higher in both immigrant groups. For the non-Western immigrants, the Gini coefficient is stable until the turn of the century. Since then, the Gini coefficient has increased strongly. This most probably reflects a strong increase in the employment rate for this group at the same time as a major share remains outside the labor market. The Gini coefficient for Western immigrants has the same profile over time as found for natives but the difference between the two groups is increasing quite strongly. An increasing number of students from Western countries might contribute to this pattern. This, however, seems to be less probable as we cut off people younger than 25 in the calculations.

Figure 16. Gini coefficients for the distribution of equivalence scale adjusted annual disposable incomes. Western, Non-Western immigrants and Natives, 1984 -2007.

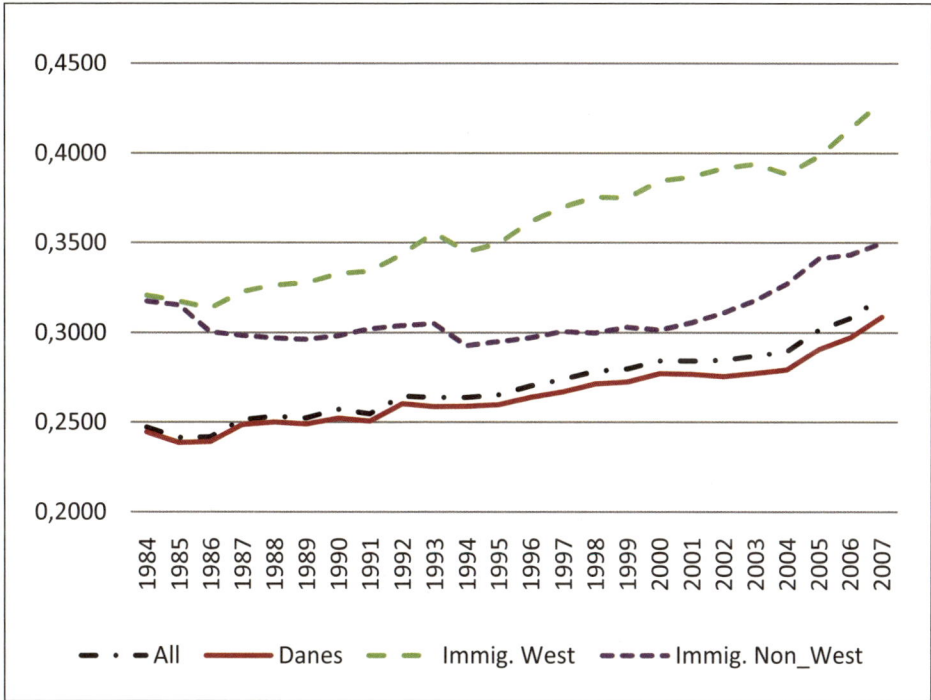

Finally, we show in Figure 17 Gini coefficients in 4 selected years over our period for immigrants from 3 non-western countries. Turkey is the only country included in all 4 years in Figure 17. Inequality is increasing throughout for the group of immigrants from Turkey. The level is however significantly below, not only the level for all non-Western immigrants, but also the level for natives, cf. Figure 16.

Figure 17. Gini coefficients for the distribution of equivalence scale adjusted annual disposable incomes. Immigrants from selected Non-Western countries in 1986, 1993, 2000 and 2007.

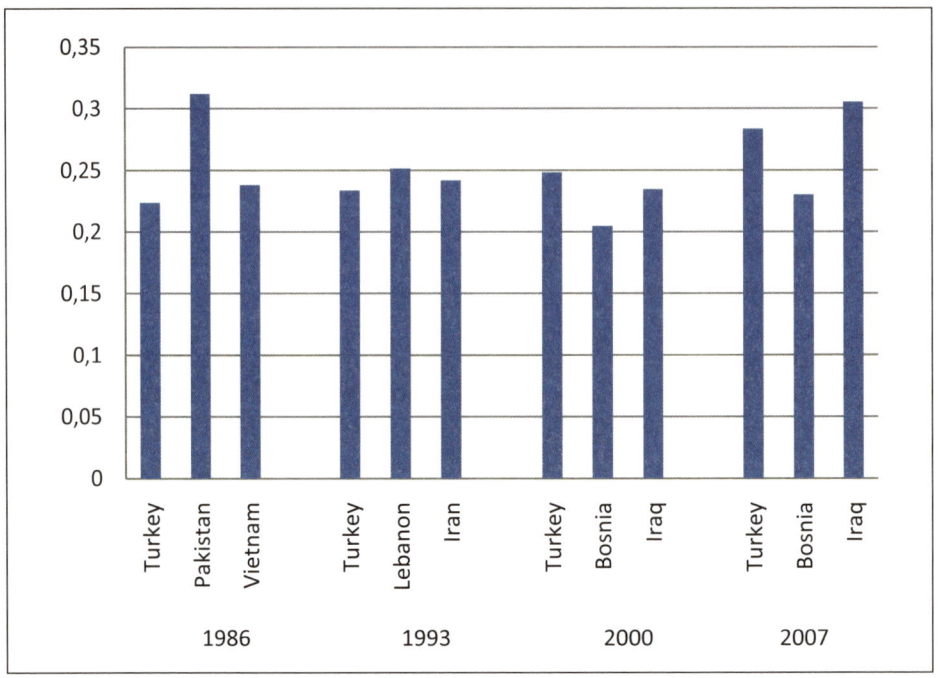

8. Conclusions

The conventional wisdom in poverty studies has been that incidence as well as duration of poverty is very low in Denmark as in the other Nordic countries. The focus above has been on the specific situation for immigrants, mostly on those coming from non-Western countries, and the main conclusion is a significant modification of the standard result regarding poverty. In Denmark it turns out that a dual society regarding poverty has come into existence. Native Danes have throughout the period a low incidence of poverty which seems to be surprisingly robust relative to the big cyclical movements since 1984. Immigrants on the other hand experience poverty to a much higher degree, out of line with conventional ideas about a Scandinavian type welfare state. There is also a big gap between immigrant and native poverty in the other Scandinavian countries. In Norway and Sweden the gap is, however, smaller than in Denmark.

Concerning annual incidence of poverty, we find as mentioned a stable and low level for natives in contrast to a strong increase for non-Western immigrants from about 30 per cent to about 50 per cent, until the poverty share stabilizes around

8. Conclusions 35

this higher level from the mid-1990s. The profile is the outcome of a complex interaction between changes in arrival patterns, countries of origin, and waves of refugees entering from the mid-1980s to the mid-1990s. High entry rates occurred at the same time as high unemployment in the domestic economy.

Explorative probit analyses of the poverty risk at 4 selected points in time shows
- an age profile for non-Western immigrants approaching the profile for natives
- a higher poverty risk for women, natives as well as immigrants
- reduced poverty risk for immigrants married to natives
- expected impact from having children, education, labor force participation and years since migration.
- and finally big differences between countries of origin for both Western and non-Western immigrants

Regarding transitions to and from poverty we find stationary entry rates for natives while it follows an inverted U shape for non-Western immigrants, reflecting changes in arrival patterns, cyclical changes and policy changes. Exit rate from poverty is high and stable for natives while it shows a step-wise decline for non-Western immigrants, decade after decade. For Western immigrants the exit rate declines, also in periods where unemployment goes down.

Persistent poverty is much more pronounced among non-Western immigrants than among natives, both when comparing distributions of the number of years spent in poverty and when converting the analysis to looking at 3 year poverty rates.

We look at income mobility by focusing on upwards mobility measured by the share of 25 – 59 years old where the equivalence scale adjusted income moves up from one year to the next from the 2. quintile in the distribution to the 4. or 5. quintile. Downwards mobility is measured as the share in the 4. quintile moving from one year to the next to the 1. or 2. quintile. Upwards mobility turns out to have been declining until the strong cyclical upswing from the turn of the century. Downwards mobility, on the other hand, has been at a stationary level for natives and for Western immigrants. For non-Western immigrants downwards mobility has a flat, inverted U-profile returning at the end of the period to the initial level. The variation between countries of origin is very big. Downwards mobility is decreasing with years since migration, although not very fast. Finally, annual Gini coefficients show higher inequality than for natives in both immigrant groups. For non-Western immigrants the Gini coefficient went up with 5 percentage points since the turn of the century. This is a reflection of increasing employment along with a big share of this population group still remaining outside the labor force. In this phase it seems, a bit counter intuitively, that higher employment reduces the poverty share at the same time as the inequality indicator goes up.

Literature

Atkinson, T., B. cantillon, E. Marlier and B. Nolan. 2002. *Social Indicators. The EU and Social Inclusion.* Oxford University Press.

Bane, M.J. and D.,T. Ellwood. 1986. Slipping into and out of poverty: the dynamics of spells. *Journal of Human Resources, 21: 1-23.*

Blume, K., B. Gustafsson, P.J. Pedersen and M. Verner. 2005. A Tale of two Countries: Poverty and Income Distribution Among Immigrants in Denmark and Sweden Since 1984, pp. 317-340 in G.J. Borjas and J. Crisp (eds.) *Poverty, International Migration and Asylum.* Palgrave. Macmillan.

Blume, K., B. Gustafsson, P.J. Pedersen and M. Verner. 2007. At the Lower End of the Table: Determinants of Poverty among Immigrants to Denmark and Sweden. *Journal of Ethnic and Migration Studies, Vol. 33, 3, 373-396.*

Bradbury, B., S.P. Jenkins and J. Micklewright. 2001a. Beyond the snapshot: a dynamic view of child poverty. Ch. 1 in Bradbury, B., S.P. Jenkins and J. Micklewright (eds.) *The Dynamics of Child Poverty in Industrialised Countries.* Unicef. Cambridge University Press.

Bradbury, B., S.P. Jenkins and J. Micklewright. 2001b. Conceptual and measurement issues. Ch. 2 in Bradbury, B., S.P. Jenkins and J. Micklewright (eds.) *The Dynamics of Child Poverty in Industrialised Countries.* Unicef. Cambridge University Press.

Cappellari, L. and S.P. Jenkins. 2004. Modelling Low Income Transitions, *Journal of Applied Econometrics,* vol. 19, 6: 593-610.

Economic Council. 2006. Fattigdom i Danmark, pp. 155-287, in Dansk Økonomi. Efterår 2006. Det Økonomiske Råd. Formandskabet. Copenhagen.

Ekberg, J. 1994. Är indvandrare fatiga? *Ekonomisk Debatt, 22, 2:169-177*

Esping-Andersen, G. 1990. *The Three Worlds of Welfare Capitalism.* Princeton University Press.

Eurofound. 2010. *Working poor in Europe.* Dublin.

Fouarge, D. and R. Layte. 2005. Welfare Regimes and Poverty Dynamics: The Duration and Recurrence of Poverty Spells in Europe. *Journal of Social Policy,* vol. 34, 3, 407-426.

Galloway, T.A. 2006. *Do immigrants integrate out of poverty in Norway?* Discussion Paper 482. Research Department of Statistics Norway.

Galloway, T.A., B. Gustafsson, P.J. Pedersen and T. Österberg. 2009. *Immigrant Child Poverty in Scandinavia: A Panel Data Study.* IZA DP No. 4232.

Hammarstedt, M. 2001. Disposable income differences between immigrants and natives in Sweden. *International Journal of Social Welfare, 10, 2: 117-126.*

Hammarstedt, M. and G.Shukur. 2007. Immigrant´s Relative Earnings in Sweden – A Quantile Regression Approach. *International Journal of Manpower, 28, 6: 456- 473.*

Juul, J.S. and G. Rosenlund. 2010. *Langvarig fattigdom er et stigende problem blandt indvandrere.* Report. Business Council of the Labor Movement. Copenhagen.

Pedersen, P.J. and N. Smith. 2000. Low Incomes in Denmark 1980-1995, Ch. 2 in B.G. Gustafsson and P.J. Pedersen (eds.) *Poverty and Low Income in the Nordic Countries.* Ashgate. Aldershot.

Pedersen, P.J. 2006. Indkomstmobilitet eller fastlåsning i lavindkomst? – Danske erfaringer 1983 til 2004, pp. 78-110 in T. Tranæs (ed.), H.J. Kleven, C.T. Kreiner, N-K. Nielsen and P.J. Pedersen. *Skat, arbejde og lighed – en undersøgelse af det danske skatte- og velfærdssystem.* Gyldendal. Copenhagen.

Pedersen, P.J. 2011. *Immigration and Welfare State Cash Benefits – The Danish Case.* The Rockwool Foundation Research Unit. Study Paper No. 33. University Press of Southern Denmark. Odense.